Mi mundo

LAS FIGURAS

Jagger Youssef

Translated by
Diana Osorio

PowerKiDS press.

New York

PK
Principiantes

¡Veo figuras!

Veo cuadrados.

Veo rectángulos.

7

Veo triángulos.

Veo círculos.

Veo óvalos.

Veo estrellas.

Veo diamantes.

Veo hexágonos.

¡Veo círculos
y rectángulos!

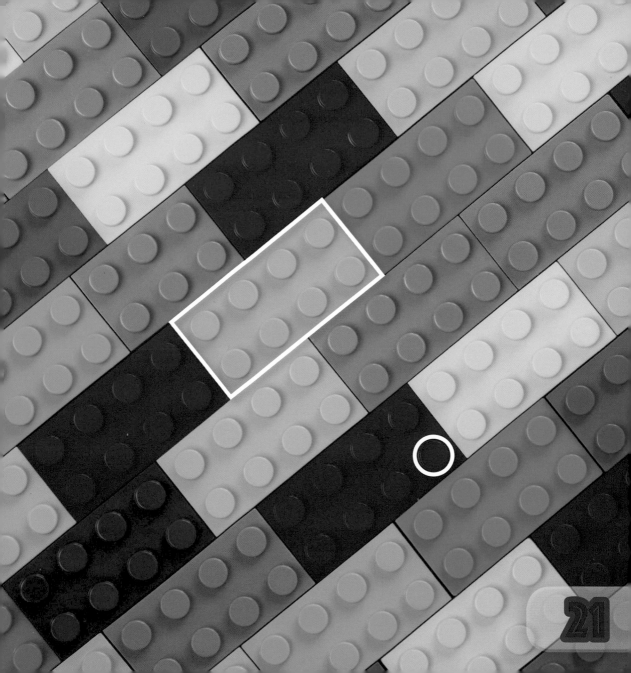

¡Las figuras
son divertidas!

Published in 2023 by The Rosen Publishing Group, Inc.
29 East 21st Street, New York, NY 10010

First Edition

Translator: Diana Osorio
Editor, Spanish: Diana Osorio
Editor, English: Therese Shea
Book Design: Michael Flynn

Photo Credits: Cover, p. 1 OnlyZoia/Shutterstock.com; back cover Max Krasnov/Shutterstock.com; p. 3 Olya Detry/Shutterstock.com; p. 5 New Africa/Shutterstock.com; p. 7 high fliers/Shutterstock.com; p. 9 Indigo Photo Club/Shutterstock.com; p. 11 Sergey Novikov/Shutterstock.com; p. 13 luca pbl/Shutterstock.com; p. 15 Agave Studio/Shutterstock.com; p. 17 kevin brine/Shutterstock.com; p. 19 yam.xyzd/Shutterstock.com; p. 21 megerka_megerka/Shutterstock.com; p. 23 Rennie Creations/Shutterstock.com.

Library of Congress Cataloging-in-Publication Data

Names: Youssef, Jagger, author.
Title: Las figuras (Shapes) / Jagger Youssef.
Description: New York : PowerKids Press, [2023] | Series: Mi mundo (My World)
Identifiers: LCCN 2021041274 (print) | LCCN 2021041275 (ebook) | ISBN
   9781538386071 (library binding) | ISBN 9781538386057 (paperback) | ISBN
   9781538386064 (set) | ISBN 9781538386088 (ebook)
Subjects: LCSH: Shapes--Juvenile literature.
Classification: LCC QA445.5 .Y68 2023 (print) | LCC QA445.5 (ebook) | DDC
   516/.15--dc23
LC record available at https://lccn.loc.gov/2021041274
LC ebook record available at https://lccn.loc.gov/2021041275

Manufactured in the United States of America

Some of the images in this book illustrate individuals who are models. The depictions do not imply actual situations or events.

CPSIA Compliance Information: Batch #CSPK23. For further information contact Rosen Publishing, New York, New York at 1-800-237-9932.

Find us on